CW00661265

Perceptions of Overcrowding

Public views of space in the home

BSHF with Rachel Moreton

Published December 2013

Cover design by www.soapbox.co.uk

ISBN 978-1-901742-49-7

This research was conducted in partnership with BSHF by Rachel Moreton, a freelance researcher.

BSHF is grateful for the contribution made by Halsall Lloyd Partnership (HLP) architects and designers, who developed the floor plans for this research on a pro-bono basis (www.hlpdesign.com).

Contents

Table of figures

Executive summary

Reducing overcrowding has been a major aim of housing policy for at least a century. There is clear evidence of a link between overcrowding and physical health conditions such as meningitis and tuberculosis. There is also evidence that overcrowding is associated with poor educational attainment, mental health problems and strained family relationships.

Overcrowding in Britain is defined in a variety of ways. An estimate made in 2003 concluded that there were approximately 20,000 overcrowded households in England according to the statutory measure.[1] However, this definition was established in 1935 and assumes that a living room can act as a bedroom. The 'bedroom standard' has been used to measure overcrowding since the 1960s. Official estimates suggest that around three per cent of households (750,000 households) in Britain are overcrowded using the bedroom standard. The 2011 Census indicates that nine per cent of households are overcrowded using a different measure – the occupancy rating.

A range of concerns exist with the current definitions of overcrowding. The use of numerous definitions makes unclear the true scale of overcrowding. Many definitions of overcrowding appear arbitrary and do not reflect differences in the way people use their homes. It is likely that perceptions of overcrowding and space in the home have changed considerably over time.

The Building and Social Housing Foundation has therefore investigated public understandings of space in the home and overcrowding using focus groups. The research explored how a minimum space standard might be meaningfully described. Focus groups concluded that a minimum standard for all households would include space for:

- **Health and development.** There should be enough space to accommodate the health needs (mental and physical) of residents and enable childhood development.

- **Social interaction.** Every home should allow space for all members of the household to eat together or for a small number of friends or family members to visit.

- **Essential items.** There should be space for essential items such as, cleaning equipment, cooking facilities and basic furniture.

There was widespread agreement across the focus groups that different types of household would have different needs in terms of health and development, social interaction and essential items. The focus groups explored these issues by developing a list of space requirements for three case study households. Participants were asked to agree the furniture and other possessions, activities and levels of privacy needed in the home. Three case study households were considered:

- **Couple with two young children.** The focus groups agreed that families with children have additional space needs, for example, to enable indoor play and store toys. The research suggests that the current age limits for children sharing bedrooms need to be reviewed.

- **Couple over 60.** Participants agreed that this type of household requires two bedrooms in order to manage the increased likelihood of ill health or disability. Other additional space needs were also identified to ensure that the home is accessible, safe and supports the needs of people as they age.

- **Single working-age man without children.** There was less agreement on the specific needs of this type of household. However, it was felt that if a person were living in a room in a shared house, there would need to be substantially more bedroom space than if a person were living in a self-contained dwelling.

The results of these discussions were used to draw up floor plans for accommodation that would provide minimum space standards for the different household types. According to the focus group discussions:

- A couple with one child require a minimum of 65 m^2 of usable floor area. In England, 14 per cent of families with children live in homes smaller than this.

- A couple over 60 require 48 m^2 of usable floor area. Currently, six per cent of couples over 60 in England live in homes smaller than this.

- A single working-age man without children requires 28 m^2 of usable floor area. At present, two per cent of single-person households in England live in homes smaller than this.

The research suggests that some current overcrowding standards fall well below public expectations, meaning that official estimates of overcrowding may be too low. There appear to be particular issues with measures of overcrowding for families. Most current overcrowding measures deem that children require less space than adults, but public perceptions suggest that children require at least as much space.

Current measures and standards based solely on rooms per person and simple age thresholds for bedroom sharing are not sufficiently sophisticated. Instead, standards need to take account of a wider range of considerations such as room size, overall usable floor space, age differences, and additional space needs related to life-stage and household composition.

In the light of these findings BSHF recommends that:

1. **The Department for Communities and Local Government, the Scottish Government and the Welsh Government should introduce a new statutory overcrowding measure that draws on public perceptions of minimum space standards.**

2. **The Department for Communities and Local Government, the Scottish Government and the Welsh Government should use the new measure to assess the scale of overcrowding, its geographic variation and its distribution amongst different household types and tenures.**

3. **Government policies on tackling overcrowding should be reviewed in the light of this updated analysis of overcrowding to ensure that they are able to tackle the scale and nature of this issue, including the introduction of new measures to tackle overcrowding as appropriate.**

4. **Social housing allocation and Housing Benefit awards should be based on this new measure. This would include altering the size criteria used in calculating the under occupancy penalty (the 'bedroom tax').**

Section 1: Impact of overcrowding

Before the First World War overcrowding was one of the biggest housing problems in Britain. The "dreadful, unsanitary and overcrowded conditions endured by millions of urban residents" were a major concern.[2] George Orwell described the scale of overcrowding in towns such as Wigan in the 1930s, where "quite often you have eight or even ten people living in a three-roomed house". With no space in the living room for a bed it meant that all of these people were "sleeping in two small rooms, probably in at most four beds".[3] Over the last century, the reduction in overcrowding has been one of the great triumphs of housing policy. The number of overcrowded households in England and Wales (according to the statutory overcrowding measure) declined from 664,000 in 1951 to 150,000 in 1976.[4]

The reduction in levels of overcrowding is a positive development due to its impact on health, education and family life.

Health

The National Institute for Health and Clinical Excellence has stated that:

> *The association between housing conditions and physical and mental ill health has long been recognised and there are a broad range of specific elements relating to housing that can affect health outcomes.*[5]

A government review concluded there is clear evidence of links between overcrowding and several aspects of ill health, including meningitis, tuberculosis and helicobacter pylori (a possible cause of gastritis, peptic ulcers and stomach cancer).[6] Studies reviewed also indicate relationships between overcrowding and respiratory disease in both children and adults. There is also evidence overcrowding has a negative impact on mental health.[7] However, the relationship between ill health and overcrowding is complex. Overcrowding and other aspects of poor housing conditions are often interlinked.

Educational attainment

In 2005 Shelter surveyed 505 overcrowded families. Respondents highlighted the fact that overcrowding made homework difficult and there was often nowhere for children to play.[8] These factors are linked with children's effective development and educational attainment. Research from France highlights the lower educational attainment of children in large families and attributes this to living in more overcrowded homes.[9] Studies in New York suggest that overcrowding has a significant detrimental impact on high school attainment levels and that the effect is particularly strong for boys.[10]

A UK government review found limited research in this area.[11] However, that which is available points to a possible relationship between overcrowding and lower educational attainment.

Family relationships

The Shelter survey also suggested that overcrowding harmed family relationships. The research provides useful insights into the practical problems resulting from overcrowding. These include uncomfortable and constantly changing sleeping arrangements, lack of privacy and no space for play or to store belongings. The report emphasises the need for separate sleeping spaces for parents and children, and for older children to have their own space.[12]

Conclusion

In summary, there is clear evidence of a link between overcrowding and physical health problems such as meningitis and tuberculosis. There is also some evidence to link overcrowding with poor educational attainment, mental health problems and strained family relationships. Despite this evidence, it is very difficult to evaluate the impacts of overcrowding robustly, particularly because overcrowding is often linked with other poor housing conditions and issues such as poverty. This is further complicated because studies use different definitions and measures of overcrowding, making comparison more difficult.

Section 2: Overcrowding in Britain

Space in the home (floor area) and crowding (the number of people per dwelling) can be measured objectively. However, determining whether a household is overcrowded is not straightforward and depends on a range of additional assumptions. These include which rooms can be used as bedrooms and which members of a household can be expected to share a bedroom. Views on these issues have changed over time and vary across cultures.[13]

A range of different measures of overcrowding are currently used in Britain. This section highlights some of the main standards and the levels of overcrowding that they estimate. Appendix 1 contains further details of overcrowding measures.

Statutory overcrowding

The statutory definition of overcrowding in Britain was introduced in the 1935 Housing Act.[14] According to this definition, household members are expected to share bedrooms with people of the same sex, irrespective of their relationship with them. The only people who should share a room with someone of the opposite sex are children under ten or adults living together as a couple. However, couples are not automatically allocated their own room; if necessary they are expected to share with another member of the household of the same sex, rather than with each other. When assessing the number of bedrooms, any suitably sized room is counted, including living rooms and kitchens.[15]

A one-off estimate made in 2003 concluded that there were approximately 20,000 overcrowded households in England, according to the statutory measure.[16] This represented around 0.1 per cent of households at the time.[17] A report from the Pro-housing Alliance highlighted how this standard is at odds with modern housing expectations:

> *In one recent case a family with two adults and eight children living in a three bedroom home, one a box room, were deemed to be only marginally overcrowded under this legislation.*[18]

Bedroom standard

The bedroom standard was developed in the 1960s for use in social surveys.[19] The number of bedrooms required is calculated according to the composition of a household and then compared with the actual number of bedrooms available. It takes account only of bedrooms rather than all rooms. The bedroom standard – which is more generous than the statutory overcrowding standard – is often used as a measure of overcrowding for policy and research purposes in Britain.[20] For example, the bedroom standard is used by local authorities in their housing allocations.[21] In 2012 the government issued new statutory guidance to local housing authorities in England on overcrowding, recommending that authorities adopt the bedroom standard as the measure of overcrowding.[22]

The estimated level of overcrowding is much higher if the bedroom standard is used rather than the statutory overcrowding measure. Official estimates suggest that around three per cent of households (750,000 households) in Britain are overcrowded using the bedroom standard (Figure 1).

Figure 1: Level of overcrowding in Britain

	Period	Percentage of households	Number of households
England[23]	2009-2012	2.9	643,000
Wales[24]	2008	2.1	26,000
Scotland[25]	2003-2006	3.7	85,000

Within these overall figures there are notable differences between tenures. Overcrowding is more common in private rented and social housing than owner occupation (six and seven per cent compared with one per cent respectively in England) with a long-term trend of increasing overcrowding for all renters (Figure 2).

Figure 2: Trends in overcrowding by tenure, three-year moving average (England)[26]

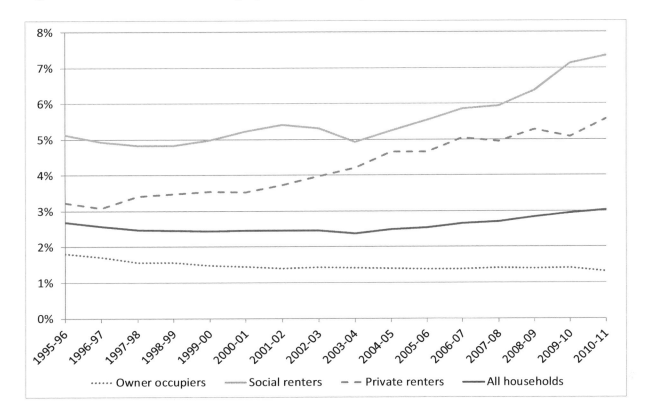

Occupancy rating

An occupancy rating is used in data from the Census to measure overcrowding and under-occupation. This measure is more generous than the bedroom standard and assumes the need for two "common rooms" (excluding bathrooms) in addition to bedrooms.[27]

The results from the 2011 Census show that in 2011 nine per cent (2.0 million) of households in England and Wales were overcrowded.[28] This is an increase of two percentage points on 2001, when seven per cent (1.5 million) of households in England and Wales were deemed to be overcrowded.

This estimate of overcrowding is much higher than those provided using other measures. The difference in estimates can be found in Figure 3. There are considerable regional differences in the rates of overcrowding estimated using the occupancy rating. The percentages of households deemed overcrowded varied from 22 per cent in London to three per cent in the South West.

Figure 3: Estimates of overcrowding using different measures

Overcrowding measure	Percentage of households (area, year)
Statutory overcrowding	0.1 (England, 2003)
Bedroom standard	2.9 (England, 2009-2012)
Occupancy rating	9 (England and Wales, 2011)

Space standards

Space standards and building regulations provide a different means of defining and understanding overcrowding.

The Parker Morris Report of 1961 is one of the most influential of these standards.[29] The recommendations were intended to apply to all housing types and were based on a consideration of lifestyle needs. These standards were based on accommodating household activities, furniture and space to move around.[30] For example, the report states that as well as a settee, chairs, small tables and a television, each living room should have enough space for other possessions such as a sewing box, toy box, radiogram and bookcase. The report was intended to provide a minimum standard for social housing.[31] However, in 1965 only 20 per cent of new council housing fully met the standard, and the standards were abandoned in 1981.[32]

In Scotland, building regulations for homes include essential space requirements for equipment, furniture and activities, including minimum kitchen storage space and space for drying clothing.[33] These standards are mandatory and apply across tenures. No equivalent building regulations currently exist for England and Wales.

In Wales, all new social housing must comply with the Development Quality Requirements, which include specifications for internal space standards.[34]

In England, social housing developments receiving funding through the National Affordable Housing Programme must meet the Homes and Community Agency's Design and Quality Standards.[35] The quality of housing is assessed by the accompanying Housing Quality Indicators. Dwellings are assessed to ensure that they accommodate specified furniture.[36] The Department for Communities and

Local Government consulted on the need for statutory minimum space standards irrespective of type of tenure in August 2013 (Box 1).

Box 1: Review of space standards in England

In August 2013, the Department for Communities and Local Government launched a consultation on housing standards for new-build accommodation. Internal space standards formed one part of this consultation. The current position was described as follows:

"National, minimum internal space standards for private sector housing have not been required in England to date, but an increasing number of planning authorities are including various different forms of space standards in local plans. The degree to which space standards should be developed or mandated is hotly contested and views for and against are very polarised".[37]

The consultation took the view that the market was generally "performing well" and stated a clear preference for "market-led solutions".[38] In order to support the functioning of the market the consultation proposed the introduction of industry wide space labelling of new homes. This would provide buyers with the overall size of the property and potentially the size of each room. The consultation also sought views on whether local authorities should be able to impose space standards as part of a Local Plan. One alternative would be to agree a national minimum space standard across England.

Housing Benefit regulations

Housing Benefit regulations also include assumptions about the amount of housing space that is required by different household types. Payments of Housing Benefit to private tenants are based on the bedroom requirement (which is similar to the bedroom standard) rather than the actual number of rooms in a claimant's home. Differences from the bedroom standard include a maximum allowance of four bedrooms, irrespective of household size. An additional room can also be included where the claimant or partner needs overnight care, and the age threshold for a separate bedroom is set at 16 (rather than 21).[39] Most single people under 35 years of age who live alone are only entitled to Housing Benefit covering the cost of renting a room in shared accommodation.[40] As of April 2013 these size criteria also apply to working-age Housing Benefit claimants in the social rented sector (Box 2).

Box 2: The under occupation penalty (the 'bedroom tax')

The Department for Work and Pensions introduced an under-occupation penalty for social housing tenants in 2013 (often referred to as the 'bedroom tax'). This means that working-age tenants in social housing will only be entitled to Housing Benefit sufficient to cover the rent on a property of the size they are assessed as needing, not their actual rent.[41] Therefore, those assessed as under-occupying their property will face a shortfall. Ministers have argued that this is to ensure equity with the private rented sector and to encourage under-occupying social tenants to downsize, freeing up larger properties for those in need.[42]

However, this policy has many detractors, with much criticism based on how the space requirements of a household are calculated.[43] For example, the requirements do not consider the size of the bedrooms; children may be required to share a bedroom even if there is insufficient space for two beds and sets of possessions.[44] Disabled children are not automatically entitled to a separate bedroom from their siblings, even though space may be needed to accommodate particular needs or specialist equipment.[45] Separated parents without permanent custody of their children are not entitled to a bedroom for them to stay in.

Three major social housing providers conducted research into households affected by this policy change.[46] Those surveyed were technically under-occupying their homes according to the size criteria above. However, over a third of these households were occupying all bedrooms. Some couples surveyed did not share a bedroom and others regularly had children to stay overnight as part of shared parenting arrangements. Other uses for spare rooms included storing equipment needed to deal with a disability or for someone working irregular shifts.

Determination of space requirements has been central to legal challenges to the policy. A tribunal ruled that box rooms could not be counted as a bedroom if they were below a minimum size.[47] One of the lawyers representing tenants argued that:

"The issue of what actually constitutes a bedroom was central to almost every case. Not only was it apparent that each case should be regarded on its merits, but that each and every room should be considered individually and that no single factor other than size could be considered to be determinative."[48]

Other concerns relating to the 'bedroom tax' include the difficulty many social tenants face in finding smaller accommodation locally and lack of flexibility with regard to changing household composition.

Problems with defining overcrowding

A range of problems exist with the current definitions of overcrowding, including issues with:

- **Assumptions.** Where overcrowding and space standards have been set, the underlying assumptions and rationale are rarely articulated. This can make the definitions seem arbitrary.[49]

- **Changing living standards.** Definitions may need updating to reflect changes in the way people use their homes: the statutory overcrowding standard was developed around 80 years ago and the bedroom standard around 50 years ago. The average household now has one more bedroom than required by the bedroom standard[50] and it has been suggested that the bedroom standard assumptions about sharing of bedrooms would now be considered to be at the margin of acceptability.[51]

- **Consideration of social norms.** The acceptability of housing space is subjective and based on social norms. However, little research explores or defines these concepts. None of the standards outlined above have been tested against public views and therefore they do not necessarily reflect what is considered socially acceptable.

- **Consistency.** The variety of definitions leads to confusion about overcrowding including the scale of the problem and its impact. Different measures provide estimates of overcrowding which range from 0.1 per cent to 9 per cent of households.

- **Insufficient detail.** The majority of the standards outlined above take into consideration only the number of bedrooms (or rooms) and do not consider the size and layout of the property, which are also likely to affect whether a household has sufficient space. In a review of the bedroom standard, local authorities argued that the space and layout (as well as number of rooms) should be taken into account.[52]

Given these complexities, it is clear that measures of overcrowding would benefit from improvement. In particular, given the importance of considering social norms and living standards, there is a need to explore public perceptions of overcrowding and space in the home. The subsequent sections consider this issue in detail.

Section 3: Public perceptions of space in the home

The previous two sections have established that overcrowding is an issue that affects a significant number of households in Britain, and has potentially serious consequences for health, development and wellbeing. However, the current measures for assessing overcrowding are inconsistent and the rationale underpinning them is unclear.

A better understanding of public perceptions of acceptable living standards would help to assess different measures of overcrowding. Therefore, the research presented here seeks to assess whether current measures of overcrowding reflect public perceptions of minimum standards of living. This section reviews current research on this topic before outlining BSHF's research, the findings of which will be detailed in the subsequent sections of this report.

A key piece of work on the subject of public perceptions of acceptable living standards was conducted for the Joseph Rowntree Foundation (JRF), in order to develop their Minimum Income Standard for Britain.[53] The research used focus groups to seek the views of the public and formulate a list of possessions, services and activities necessary to meet a minimum acceptable standard of living in Britain today. The cost of these was then calculated by a panel of experts in order to arrive at a minimum weekly income for a range of household types. Overcrowding and space in the home were not explored in detail, but housing types were identified for different household compositions (Figure 4).[54] These minimum housing requirements were then used to derive basic housing costs such as rent, council tax and fuel.

Figure 4: Appropriate housing for different household types, Minimum Income Standard definitions

Family type	Dwelling
Single adult	1-bed, mid-terrace, ground-floor flat
Couple, no children	2-bed, ground-floor flat
Single pensioner	1-bed, mid-terrace, ground-floor flat
Couple pensioner	2-bed, ground-floor flat
Lone parent, 1 child (toddler)	2-bed, end-terrace house
Couple, 2 children (pre-school, primary school)	3-bed, mid-terrace
Couple, 3 children (pre-school, primary school, secondary school)	4-bed house

In contrast with current overcrowding measures couples were considered to need two bedrooms (current measures permit one) and families were given enough bedrooms for each child to sleep separately (current measures expect some children in households to share bedrooms).

While the JRF Minimum Income Standard research provides some useful insights into public views on overcrowding and space in the home, it is limited in scope, as the emphasis of the research project was on income as opposed to space. Therefore, BSHF has conducted research that focuses on the issue of space in the home, using a similar approach to that adopted by JRF.

The BSHF research used focus groups to obtain the views of a range of members of the public. Focus groups enabled discussion amongst participants, which often clarified the views of individuals and allowed some groups to move towards a consensus on particular issues.

A series of focus groups were held in towns and cities in the East Midlands region of England. These groups discussed minimum space requirements for the permanent homes of different household types.

As a basis for the discussion, the focus groups used the definition of minimum standards that was developed by the Minimum Income Standard research:

> *"A minimum standard of living in Britain today includes, but is more than just, food, clothes, shelter. It is about having what you need in order to have the opportunities and choices necessary to participate in society".*[55]

Each of the groups discussed what this minimum space standard would be for:

* Furniture and other possessions required by households
* Activities that a household would need to undertake in the home
* Levels of privacy needed for wellbeing

In determining what furniture and activities there should be space for, participants were also informed that this did not necessarily mean every household should own these items, just have space for them.

Participants were asked to consider the needs of one of three case study households: a single working-age man without children, a couple with two young children, and a couple aged over 60. Focus groups discussed the case study household that was most similar to their own profile (e.g. focus groups made up of people over 60 discussed the case study of the couple aged over 60). These household types were similar to those used in the Minimum Income Standard research.

From the discussions, a list was drawn up of activities and possessions that the groups considered essential for each household to have space for. These lists were translated into floor plans for each household to calculate minimum floor areas required for the households. The findings of the research are presented in the subsequent sections.

Further details on the focus group method can be found in Appendix 2.

Section 4: Space needs for all households

The focus groups first discussed what they felt was meant by a minimum standard of living, guided by the initial definition provided by the researcher. A number of basic survival needs were recognised by the focus groups and generally provoked little debate or disagreement. It was agreed that a home should provide space to sleep, eat and drink, and keep clean and warm. In addition, almost all focus group participants agreed that a minimum standard of living today went beyond these things. Access to services, education, health, privacy and social interaction were highlighted as important aspects of a minimum standard of living.

A number of recurring themes emerged from the focus groups. The focus group discussions suggested that a minimum standard for households would include space for:

- Health and development
- Social interaction
- Essential possessions and items of furniture
- Flexibility and variation

Health and development

It was widely agreed across the focus groups that homes should have enough space to accommodate the health needs (mental and physical) of residents and enable childhood development. Examples included ensuring that there was enough space for children to play safely, to accommodate ill health or limited mobility (particularly for older people) and to allow room for simple exercises such as press-ups or yoga.

Many participants felt that a lack of space was not conducive to mental wellbeing. Participants spoke of how too small a home could be claustrophobic, stressful or restrictive. Phrases such as "it would drive me mad" were often used to describe having insufficient space in the home. One aspect of this was the importance of individuals having their "own space". This was often in relation to being able to retreat or "get away" from other people in the household and their activities. Examples included parents having a break from children, children having a territory that was "theirs", escaping housemates in shared accommodation and family members being able to retreat from confrontations.

Social interaction

A key part of the definition of a minimum standard of living is that it enables people to participate in society. The ability to maintain social, family and working lives were all considerations raised by participants when deciding how much space was needed in the home.

> *For me, my criteria for essential was that, firstly you had to ensure someone maintains their health and wellbeing, so in a sense they need to be able to work, to keep healthy and have social interaction. So it was geared around those requirements. (Nottingham)*

Participants from across the focus groups described social interaction as an important part of a minimum standard of living. This included allowing space for a small number of visitors to sit down and share a drink or meal, undertake hobbies and enjoy basic forms of entertainment such as watching television. Opportunities for socialising in order to avoid isolation were particularly important for older focus group participants.

Another aspect of social interaction was the need for space to prepare for commitments outside the home. For working-age participants this focused on having space to get ready for work (e.g. ironing clothes), to store work clothes or materials and work at home (at a table or using a laptop). For parents this meant children having space to complete their homework and store schoolbooks.

Essential possessions and items of furniture

There was widespread agreement amongst groups that there should be enough space in the home for essential possessions and items of furniture. However, participants expressed a range of opinions on which items were considered essential. Dishwashers, for example, were said to be non-essential, while a microwave was agreed to be not only convenient but cheap, efficient, space-saving and "most people" have them in Britain today. Details of these discussions are provided in the next section.

Participants from all groups highlighted the importance of space for storage. Space under the stairs, in lofts and in airing cupboards was clearly valued and useful in keeping certain possessions "out of the way", avoiding mess and clutter. Participants in one group talked about the impact that a lack of storage space has on perceptions of the home:

*So if you've got your clothes ... say you've got a double wardrobe like that
big one you can hang your clothes up and it's all neat and it makes you feel
better and calmer, whereas if you've got a little wardrobe and then you've
got everything crammed in, it makes you feel a bit like "ooh I don't feel
nice". (Lincoln)*

Participants suggested ways in which limited space might be cleverly used. This
included use of folding tables and chairs, under-bed drawers and stackable
storage boxes. Some items, it was argued, could have multiple uses. For example,
dining tables could be used for homework and dining chairs can be used to seat
visitors. Some items, such as a shower (as opposed to a bath) and a fridge-freezer
(as opposed to separate units) were recommended because they use space
efficiently.

Participants also discussed how people living in a minimum standard home were
likely to be on low incomes and that this was an important consideration for
space. For example, some also felt space for a television was not essential, as they
could be wall-mounted. However, most participants agreed that space for an
older style "big" television was needed as "not everyone can afford flat ones".
One participant pointed out that a low-income family might also need more
space to store hand-me-down baby equipment.

Flexibility and variation

"It depends" was a frequent refrain in discussions. Participants emphasised that
every household is different and would have different needs. The need for space
in the home was variously said to depend on age, gender, lifestyle, family
structure and dynamics, expectations, local area, culture, individual personality,
job and personal relationships. This led to some participants expressing concern
about having standards that were too rigid and did not allow flexibility to meet
individual needs and preferences. For example, some suggested that elements
such as bike storage or outside space might not be needed by all but that
everyone should have the option to have these things if wanted.

This led to the conclusion that minimum standards were not about prescribing a
particular use of space within the home. Instead, the minimum standard was
intended to provide the smallest amount of space within which a household
could be expected to live healthy lives, maintain social interaction and
accommodate essential possessions and furniture. Different households would be
expected to use this space in different ways to reflect their own priorities and
lifestyle.

Section 5: Space needs for different household types

The focus groups agreed that different household types would have different needs. This issue was investigated further by developing a list of space requirements for the three case study households. Participants were asked to agree the furniture, possessions, activities and levels of privacy needed in the home.

The case studies focused discussions on specific circumstances and provided a common basis for discussion across groups. The case studies were also useful in steering the discussion away from focusing on the individual personal preferences of focus group members.

The following case study households were used:

- Couple with two young children: The Davies family. Paul and Sarah have two children. Jack is four and his sister, Olivia, is three months.

- Couple over 60: John and Christine have been married for 45 years and are both now retired. John is 75 and Christine is 69.

- Single working-age man without children: Tom, aged 30.

Couple with young children

Focus groups of families with children were asked to agree minimum space requirements for the Davies family: Paul and Sarah, and their children Jack (four) and Olivia (three months).

Bedroom sharing

Family focus groups explored the issue of bedroom sharing with regard to the case study family but also discussed the issue more generally. The focus groups agreed that a two-bedroom home was adequate for the Davies family in their present form, but that a third bedroom would be needed soon, although the timescales and reasoning for this varied from group to group.

Participants from all the family groups were happy for Olivia (three months) to share a bedroom with her parents for the time being. Some suggested that for the first few months sharing a room with parents is beneficial and recommended. Current NHS recommendations are for babies to be in the same room as parents when they are asleep, day and night for the first six months.[56] The view in most of these groups was that sharing a bedroom is acceptable for six to 12 months only. Participants were concerned about the impact on parental privacy.

> *I'd say up to six months, because after that you're going to be creeping around, and that might like... if the man and wife want to do something they're not going to be able to because the baby is going to be in the cot looking, so, do you know what I mean? Everyone needs their space, whether they're a month old, six months old to adults. (Lincoln)*

Simply moving Olivia in with her older brother Jack was seen as a contentious solution, despite the fact that both children are of an age when current overcrowding standards say it is acceptable for two children of different sexes to share. Participants in two groups expressed safety concerns about a child of Jack's age sharing with a baby.

> *I was told by the health visitor [...] never to leave the toddler alone with the baby, because they could just do daft things, they could throw a pillow in or something. (Nottingham)*

Participants were also concerned about the potential for Olivia to disturb Jack's sleep and highlighted that this could become more of a problem when Jack starts school.

> *You know, the baby's going to be awake all night, the poor chap can't get his sleep for school, he's not going to concentrate at school... (Derby)*

Initial suggestions as to the age threshold when bedroom sharing for children of different sex was no longer acceptable ranged from two to ten. After discussion, there was broad agreement in all groups that the age limit was around seven years. This is younger than commonly found in overcrowding standards.

Getting agreement on the acceptability of children of the same sex sharing a bedroom was more difficult. Opinions on the age limit for same-sex sharing tended to fall into two groups, suggesting either around ten or 18 years of age.

Again, the need for privacy associated with children growing up and personal space, along with averting arguments, were given as reasons why even children of the same sex, at some point, need a room of their own.

*From my own personal experience ... me and my brother ... we were put in together until quite late, so I think it needs to be brought down to be honest with you, 'cause you can... it's not like it were good for my parents to be honest with you, because me and him were rowing all the time.
(Nottingham)*

The age gap between children was raised as a relevant consideration here. Some participants added a caveat that the acceptability of same-sex sharing was dependent on the children being of a similar age. A greater age gap between children was said to make sharing less acceptable.

I said any age, but it depends what the age difference is. So if you've got say a 16 year old boy and a seven year old boy I don't think it's quite appropriate. (Derby)

Participants in two different groups also suggested the size of the bedroom should be taken into account, suggesting that bunk beds might not always be suitable.

As long as they've got enough space within that room; not a little box room. You can't have like say two teenagers and they're in their bunk beds because there's no space. (Lincoln)

The bedroom standard does not allow a separate bedroom for an individual until they are 21.

Participants were often reluctant to set overarching rules on bedroom sharing based on age thresholds alone. They highlighted various other considerations that they felt needed to be taken into account when it came to the acceptability of both mixed- and same-sex sharing. Participants suggested a disability, the individual child's temperament, family dynamics and effects on schooling were all possible factors that might make children sharing a bedroom more or less acceptable for different families.

I think [age] seven as a general rule, but it's got to be taken into account any problems there are in the family, or any... because a lot of it, if you get [a] brother and sister who get on really well and there's no problems and then you get kids who fight all the time. (Derby)

Assumptions about the acceptability of bedroom sharing for children form a key part of overcrowding standards. The evidence from this research suggests that current social norms may be different from overcrowding standards. It also reveals the complexity of the issue and that a simple age limit does not always cover all concerns.

Family life

The family focus group participants also identified a number of specific space requirements relating to children and the ability to maintain an acceptable family life. All family groups agreed that space for a table for the family to sit and eat together was important for family relationships and as a place to teach good manners. The following exchange is typical.

> Participant A: *I'd say that's essential [space for a table] because it's more and more becoming apparent that if families eat together...*
> Participant B: *Work together, don't they?*
> Participant A: *Yeah, it helps them sort of work together and talk and discuss and I think it's essential.*
> Participant C: *And also it's about education isn't it, dinner time? It's about teaching children good table manners, you know, appropriate ways to eat. (Nottingham)*

In the absence of additional space for a desk, it was also suggested the dining table could be useful space for homework.

> *Parents can sit with them while they're doing their homework and supervise them. If [children are] in their room, you don't know whether they are doing it properly. (Derby)*

Participants talked about the "clutter" that comes with having small children in particular, such as nappies and toys. Participants all agreed that it was important to have space to store toys and additional floor space for children to play; especially for the Davies family with two very young children. One participant suggested this space might later be used for a desk as the children grew up. Participants made clear that they wanted space for a travel-system pushchair that can cater for children from newborn upwards. This type of pushchair was said to be bulky but having space for one was agreed to be essential.

Almost all participants who discussed this issue felt space for indoor play and for setting out items like bouncy chairs or a changing mat for the baby were important.

> *I mean, they need floor space don't they. I mean he's going to play with cars isn't he on the floor. [...] Because children do tend to play on the floor at that age don't they. (Derby)*

Participants were also unanimous that space for a washing machine for the Davies family was essential.

Definitely with small children ... You never stop washing. (Derby)

Box 3 shows the full list of minimum space needs for the Davies family as agreed by the family focus group participants.

Box 3: Minimum space requirements for a couple with two young children

Type of home

- Two bedrooms adequate now, but three bedrooms needed soon

Parents' bedroom

Space for...

- Double bed
- Four-door wardrobe or two two-door wardrobes
- Two chests of drawers

Children's bedrooms

Space for...

- Single bed (per child)
- Two-door wardrobe (per child)
- Chest of drawers (per child)

Other child-related (not necessarily in their bedrooms)

Space for...

- Cupboard/shelving for toys (per child)
- Travel system pushchair
- Clear floor space for play (approximately 2 m²)

Bathroom

Space for...

- Toilet
- Basin
- Bath
- Bathroom cabinet

Living space

Space for...

- Comfortable seating for four people
- Table for four people with four chairs
- Television (older style, not wall-mounted) on stand
- Sideboard/dresser

Kitchen

Space for...

- Sink
- Cooker
- Microwave
- Fridge-freezer
- Washing machine
- Work surface for small appliances (kettle, toaster, bottle steriliser) and food preparation
- Four double cupboards plus under-sink cupboard
- Large waste bin

Other storage

Space for...

- Cupboard for vacuum, ironing board, mop/bucket, dustpan and brush.
- Shoes and coats
- Items not in everyday use (e.g. Christmas decorations, suitcases, and baby equipment) although this could be in an outside store or attic (if available)

Couple over 60

The focus groups of adults over 60 were asked to agree minimum space requirements for John and Christine, who have been married for 45 years and are both retired. John is 75 and Christine is 69.

Bedroom space

All the over-60s focus groups agreed that, as a minimum, there should be at least two bedrooms for the couple. This was justified mainly because of the increased likelihood of ill health or disability. These issues were seen to require extra space which could either allow a carer to stay overnight, provide time and space needed for recovery or to give the partner a break.

> *I think that's a must [a second bedroom] because ... if one is ill and the other one can't cope or the one that is ill can't cope with someone near them you must have another room. You must. (Chesterfield)*

> *If you're suffering from ill health and your wife's looking after you, you've got to have quality time. (Nottingham)*

Other reasons given for why John and Christine need a second bedroom included being able to accommodate overnight visits from family and having additional storage space.

The agreed space requirements for the main bedroom were broadly similar across all the over-60s focus groups, and included a double bed, two two-door wardrobes, one or two chests of drawers, bedside cabinets and a chair.

There was agreement across the over-60s focus groups that the second bedroom need only be a single bedroom or box room. Only one group discussed the detail of what this room should accommodate and the results were broadly in line with the requirements identified by the working-age focus groups for the bedroom for a single working-age man living in a one-bedroom flat.

Accessibility and safety

Additional space needs were identified to ensure that the home was accessible, safe and supported the needs of John and Christine as they age. Accessibility and facilitating everyday living for people who may be less fit and able were frequently raised as justifications for having space for certain items. For example, space for a chair in the bedroom to help with getting dressed, and a coffee table in the living room so a hot drink can be placed safely within reach were both felt to be necessary.

Participants felt that space for a freezer (rather than an icebox in the top of a fridge) was essential for John and Christine. It was said to be important in order to reduce the frequency of shopping trips, particularly if one of the couple is unwell, or there are poor weather conditions.

> *Like last year when I couldn't get out I emptied my freezer nearly in the end, because you can't get out but you've got enough stuff in your freezer to live. (Leicester)*

Participants also highlighted that older people might have a supply of frozen meals delivered (an alternative to hot 'meals on wheels'), for which a full-sized freezer (and microwave) are essential.

> *People in this area, I don't know if it's the same everywhere, use [name of supplier]. And they come with pre-packed stuff, it goes straight in the freezer, then straight in the microwave and it's really, really good stuff. Therefore you've got to have a freezer in those situations. (Chesterfield)*

Participants in one of the over-60s focus groups suggested that space for a folded wheelchair, walker or similar mobility aid was essential. It was argued that such items were widely used and could take up a lot of space. A shower, rather than a bath, was agreed to be a suitable minimum by all these groups and almost all participants viewed this as preferable because of the increased accessibility it affords. Participants were also concerned that there should be sufficient space and storage to avoid the home becoming cluttered and increasing the risk of trips and falls.

The full requirements for John and Christine as identified by the over-60s focus groups are outlined in Box 4.

Box 4: Minimum space requirements for a couple over 60

Type of home

- Two bedrooms (one double, one single)
- A home on one level (either a bungalow or a flat, not above second storey level)

Bedroom 1

Space for...

- Double bed
- Four-door wardrobe or two two-door wardrobes
- Chest of drawers
- Small chair
- Two bedside cabinets

Bedroom 2

Space for...

- Single bed
- Two-door wardrobe
- Bedside cabinet

Bathroom

Space for...

- Toilet
- Basin
- Walk in shower with fold-down seat inside.
- Bathroom cabinet

Living space

Space for...

- Comfortable seating for two people
- Dining table for two (with ability to extend for four) with two chairs
- Nest of tables
- Display/storage unit
- Bookcase
- Television (older style, not wall-mounted) on stand

Kitchen

Space for...

- Sink
- Cooker
- Microwave
- Fridge freezer
- Washing machine (unless there is access to a shared laundry as part of a retirement complex or similar)
- Work surface sufficient to keep a kettle and toaster on and to prepare food
- Four cupboards (including under-sink)

Other storage

Space for...

- Vacuum cleaner, ironing board, mop and bucket, etc
- Coats and shoes by the door
- Any mobility aids or specialist medical equipment
- Items not in everyday use (e.g. suitcases and decorations), although this could be in the second bedroom or attic (if available)

Single household

Groups of working-age participants without children were asked to discuss the minimum space requirements for Tom, who is 30, single and has no children.

Type of home

These participants were unable agree the type of housing that was acceptable as a minimum for Tom; in particular, whether that be a self-contained flat, shared accommodation or living with his parents. For the purpose of this exercise a self-contained dwelling without shared facilities was assumed, as this made it easier to determine the space that Tom alone required (as opposed to his needs as part of a larger household).

"Getting by"

Some participants referred to their own experiences of being able to "get by" without certain items such as fridge-freezers or washing machines, particularly those living in student accommodation. This may be because such lifestyles are not seen as permanent or long-term, as one participant observed:

> *I think we could all, like, get by but ... I wouldn't like to be living in my style of housing when I'm thirty. (Leicester)*

Participants were also more likely to suggest that some needs could be met outside the home, such as a visiting a launderette or using a computer at a library.

Whether or not to include space for a washing machine proved problematic for participants. Some felt a washing machine to be a luxury item and that a single person could easily use a launderette or even wash clothes at home by hand. Others highlighted the inconvenience of this, especially for busy working people, and the fact that launderettes may not be available everywhere.

> *I don't think it's acceptable if a person should have to walk a mile and a half across town to wash their clothes. Perhaps if they live really nearby to one then it's a bit more acceptable. I think if there isn't one nearby then there should be a washing machine. Someone should be able to do their clothes when they want. (Kettering)*

Overall, the balance of opinion across groups was more in favour than against, and space for a washing machine has been included in the list of necessities.

Flexible space

Participants felt it was important that there was space for a small dining table and chairs, even if an individual then decided to use the space differently.

> *I think it's important to have the choice, if you choose to do that with your space, because you know, I know a lot of people do eat on their laps, but with digestion and that, being able to eat properly it is better for them to eat at the table, and I think if someone doesn't have the chance to do that, it's not really meeting that description [of a minimum standard of living].*
> *(Kettering)*

Participants felt that having space for a table also provided a space to work or study. In common with other groups, working-age people without children did not feel space for a desktop computer was necessary because laptops were common and saved space.

The full list of agreed minimum space needs for Tom is shown in Box 5.

Box 5: Minimum requirements for a single, working-age man with no children

Type of home

- One-bedroom flat

Bedroom

Space for...

- Single bed
- Two-door wardrobe
- Chest of drawers

Bathroom

Space for...

- Toilet
- Basin
- Shower
- Bathroom cabinet

Living space

Space for...

- Comfortable seating for two people
- Table for two people with two chairs
- Wall-mounted shelves
- Television (older style, not wall-mounted) on stand or coffee table
- Floor space for setting up a clothes horse, exercising or prayer

Kitchen

Space for...

- Sink
- Cooker (or mini-oven with two hotplates and microwave)
- Under-counter fridge-freezer
- Washing machine (or access to an onsite laundry)
- Two cupboards plus under-sink cupboard
- Work surface for food preparation and a kettle
- Bin

Other storage

- Space for a vacuum cleaner and ironing board, but not necessarily a separate cupboard
- Access to secure bike store

Section 6: Floor plans for minimum standard accommodation

The results of the focus group discussions were used to draw up floor plans for accommodation that would meet the minimum space standards identified. Halsall Lloyd Partnership (HLP), an interdisciplinary architecture and design business, drew up floor plans for each scenario. As well as the furniture and activities identified by the focus groups, the layouts included space for circulation, doors, windows and space needed for natural furniture layouts. An allowance for radiators was also included, making sure they were not covered by furniture. These layouts were then used to calculate the minimum floor areas required to meet the minimum standards agreed by the focus groups.

Couple with young children

There are two different plans for this case study, reflecting the changing needs of the case study household, as the children grow. The plans are for a two-bedroom three-person house with space for a cot in the main bedroom (Figure 5); and a three-bedroom four-person house suitable for the growing Davies family (Figure 6).

Based on the list of items and activities drawn up by the family focus group participants, the usable internal floor area needed for the two-bedroom, three-person house (Figure 5) is 64.8 m^2. By comparison, the Parker Morris Standard for a three-person house is 56.7 m^2, although it is assumed that the dwelling is either a flat or bungalow.[57] Parker Morris standards are based on a net internal floor area, which is equivalent to usable rather than gross internal area.

According to the English Housing Survey, 13.8 per cent of couples with dependent children live below this standard.[a] This compares with only 7.3 per cent of this household type being considered overcrowded by the bedroom standard. This suggests that the rate of overcrowding could be almost double current estimates when public perceptions are taken into account.

[a] References in this section to the English Housing Survey are based on authors' calculations using the raw data from the Homes component of the 2010 edition of the survey, which can be obtained from http://discover.ukdataservice.ac.uk/catalogue/?sn=7040&type=Data%20catalogue.

Figure 5: Floor plan for two-bed three-person house[b]

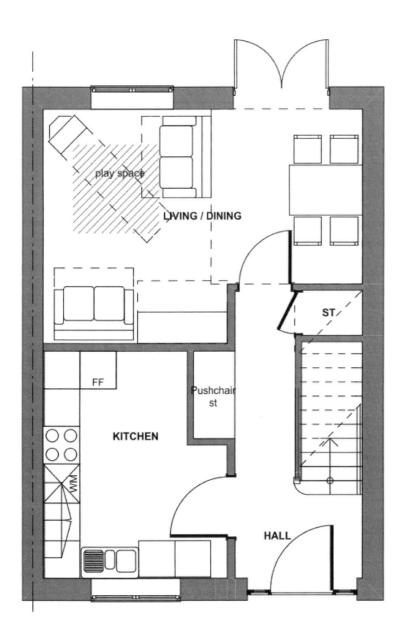

Ground floor

---

[b] ST = storage space; FF = fridge-freezer; WM = washing machine

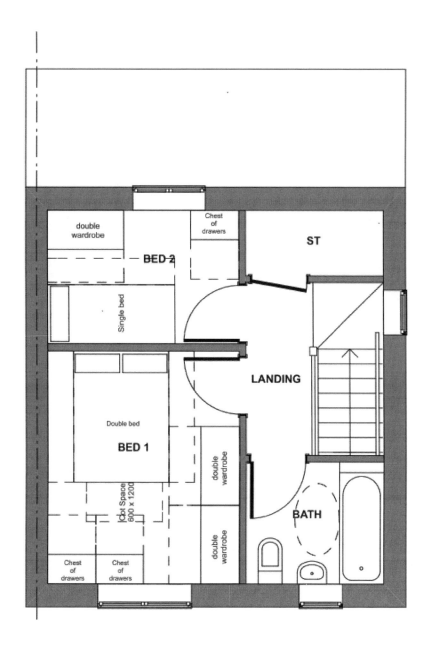

First floor

The usable internal floor area needed for the three-bedroom, four-person house (Figure 6) is 73.7m². By comparison, the Parker Morris Standard for a four-person house is 71.5 m², based on the property being a semi-detached or end terrace.[58] English Housing Survey data show that 27.4 per cent of households containing a couple with dependent children live below this standard. However, this figure includes couples with one child, who would not need as much space as allowed for in this plan. This compares with only 7.3 per cent of couples with children being overcrowded according to the bedroom standard.

The minimum requirements lists agreed by family focus groups indicate that children over about one year require as much space as an adult for sleeping. The minimum bedroom size for a single child based on this research is 6.9 m². The statutory overcrowding standard suggests that children under ten can sleep in bedrooms of just 4.7 m². The bedroom standard does not stipulate a minimum size for bedrooms.

Figure 6: Floor plan for three-bed, four-person house

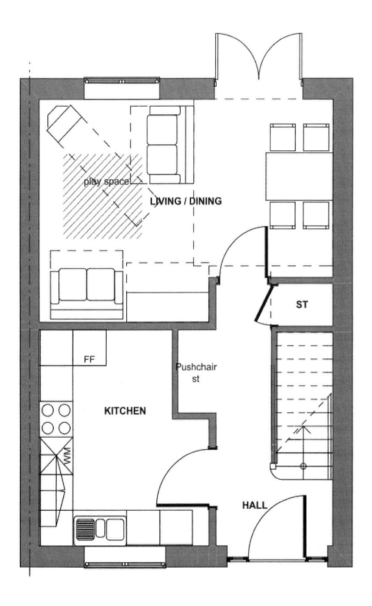

Ground floor

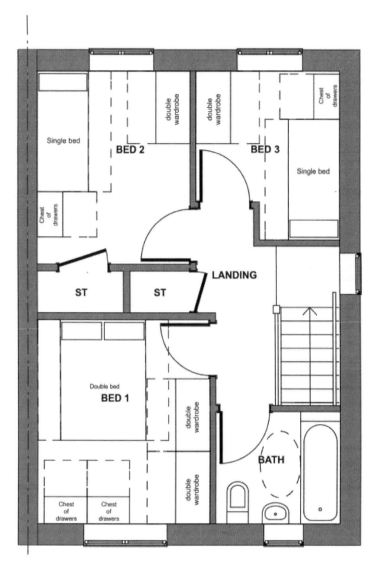

First floor

Couple over 60

The layout for a two-bedroom bungalow or flat that would meet the minimum requirements for a couple over 60 is shown in Figure 7.

The minimum usable internal floor area is 48.3 m^2. By comparison, the Parker Morris Standard for a two-person flat or bungalow is 44.6 m^2.[59] Data from the English Housing Survey show that 5.8 per cent of couples over 60 with no dependent children live in accommodation smaller than that proposed in the above plans. This compares with only 0.3 per cent of two-person households over 60 being considered overcrowded according to the bedroom standard.

Furthermore four per cent of couples over 60 with no other family members (approximately 138,000 households) are living in dwellings with only one bedroom. However, none of these households are classed as overcrowded under the bedroom standard, as one bedroom per couple is considered adequate.

Figure 7: Floor plan for two-bed two-person bungalow/flat

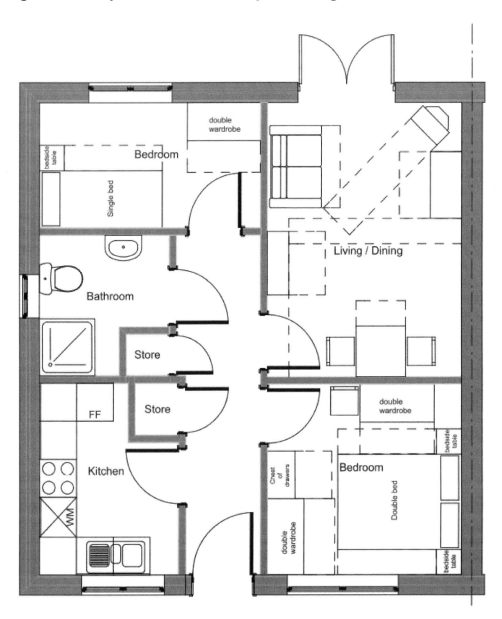

Single household

A possible layout for a single-occupant, one-bed flat that would meet the minimum requirements agreed by the relevant focus groups is outlined in Figure 8. The suggested minimum usable internal floor area needed to accommodate all the furniture and activities identified is 27.8 m². By comparison, the Parker Morris Standard for a one-person flat or bungalow is 29.7 m².[60]

Data from the English Housing Survey show that 2.2 per cent of working-age single-person households live in homes smaller than that proposed in the plans. However, this percentage is calculated from a small sample size and may not, therefore, be representative. It is perhaps unsurprising that only a small percentage of single-person households live in smaller accommodation than the plans, as 64 per cent of working-age single-person households live in homes with more than one bedroom, which are likely to be larger than the minimum standard. Based on current standards, a single person cannot be overcrowded, irrespective of the size of the dwelling they occupy, as standards consider only the number of bedrooms needed, without reference to other space needs.

Figure 8: Floor plan for one-bed flat

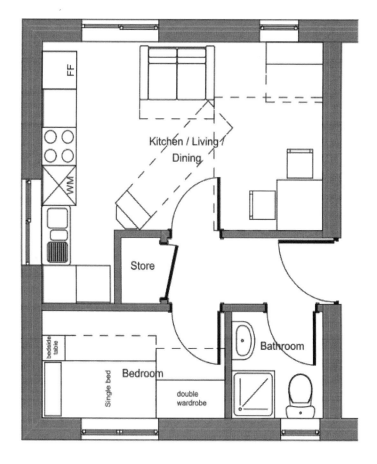

Based on the lists drawn up by participants, the minimum floor area required was 5.4 m^2 for a single adult and 6.9 m^2 for a child. Although this is the reverse of what might be expected, the single working-age adult lives alone and so can use the entire dwelling and does not need the bedroom for privacy, whereas in a multi-person household, bedrooms can be important for privacy and storing possessions. Participants noted that if Tom were to live in shared accommodation, he would need a larger bedroom to gain privacy and possibly to spend time with guests. Therefore, the small bedroom size for Tom may be misleading in this case.

Summary of findings

The evidence presented in the floor plans emphasises the discrepancy between current overcrowding standards and the minimum space in the home considered acceptable by the focus group participants. The majority of current standards do not consider the size of bedrooms and none consider overall dwelling size. The findings presented here suggest that this is an important oversight. Figure 9 summarises the findings of the research, comparing the bedroom standard overcrowding measure with the measures developed by the focus groups, for each of the case study households.

Figure 9: Summary of findings

Case study	Usable internal floor area (m^2)	Overcrowded (%) according to the bedroom standard	Overcrowded (%) according to focus group definitions
Couple with one child (2-bed)	64.8	7.3[c]	13.8
Couple with two children (3-bed)	73.7	7.3[d]	27.4[d]
Couple over 60	48.3	0.3	5.8
Single working-age person	27.8	0	2.2

[c] The English Housing Survey data do not indicate number of children so the figure here in both cases is for a household with one or more children.
[d] This figure is based on the percentage of all households with children living in accommodation smaller than the standard. However, this therefore includes households with one child, who would only be deemed to be living below an acceptable minimum if their accommodation was smaller than 64.8 m^2. Therefore, this figure is somewhat inflated.

Section 7: Conclusions and recommendations

Conclusions

The focus groups highlighted a number of important findings about perceptions of minimum standards. For example:

- Bedroom sharing between children should end at lower ages than is currently provided for by most overcrowding measures.

- Families with children have additional space needs, to enable healthy development and family life.

- A couple over 60 needs at least two bedrooms to accommodate changing health needs.

- There are additional space needs for a couple over 60 to ensure the home is accessible and safe, and supports the needs of people as they age.

This suggests that present overcrowding standards do not meet current public expectations of minimum standards. Current estimates of overcrowding at around three per cent of households are likely to be too low. This is particularly true for families where a much higher proportion of households – between 14 and 25 per cent – would be deemed overcrowded based on public perceptions.

Furthermore, measures and standards based solely on rooms per person and simple age thresholds for bedroom sharing do not appear to be sufficiently sophisticated. Instead, standards need to account for a wider range of considerations such as room size, overall usable floor space, age differences, life-stage and household composition.

Recommendations

All households should be able to access accommodation that meets minimum space needs, irrespective of household type, tenure or location. The findings presented here suggest that the public do not consider current standards as accurately assessing those needs. In the light of these findings, BSHF recommends that:

1. **The Department for Communities and Local Government, the Scottish Government and the Welsh Government should introduce a new statutory overcrowding measure that draws on public perceptions of minimum space standards.**

It is widely agreed that the statutory overcrowding measure is outdated. The findings presented here suggest that the bedroom standard also fails to meet modern expectations. Therefore, the administrations in England, Scotland and Wales should introduce a new statutory overcrowding measure that is in line with modern expectations. This measure should include reference to the sizes of rooms, ensuring that households have sufficient space for essential possessions and activities, as well as privacy from other household members.

2. **The Department for Communities and Local Government, the Scottish Government and the Welsh Government should use the new measure to assess the scale of overcrowding, its geographic variation and its distribution amongst different household types and tenures.**

3. **Government policies on tackling overcrowding should be reviewed in the light of this updated analysis of overcrowding to ensure that they are able to tackle the scale and nature of this issue, including the introduction of new measures to tackle overcrowding as appropriate.**

4. **Social housing allocation and Housing Benefit awards should be based on the new statutory measure. This would include altering the size criteria used in calculating the under-occupancy penalty (the 'bedroom tax').**

Further research

More research is required to develop the findings of this exploratory study. This could seek to investigate:

- **The needs of different household types.** For example, lone parents, parents with children who only live with them some of the time, extended family households and single people sharing accommodation.

- **The additional needs of larger households.** The likelihood of being overcrowded increases sharply when the number of people in a household reaches five or more.[61]

- **More detailed analysis of bedroom sharing.** For example, what factors are important in considering the acceptability of bedroom sharing in addition to age and sex?

- **Minimum standards for single people.** There was less agreement among the focus group participants on the types of minimum accommodation for this group. Is it possible to agree a maximum age for shared accommodation? Are there particular groups (e.g. those with specific health needs) who should not be required to live in shared accommodation?

Answering these questions would aid the development of a new overcrowding standard that is fit for purpose and meets public perceptions of acceptable living standards. This would provide additional clarity to the findings presented here.

Appendix 1: Definitions of overcrowding

This Appendix provides greater detail on existing definitions of overcrowding, building on the information outlined in Section 2.

Statutory overcrowding standard[62]

The statutory overcrowding standard comprises two standards, a room standard and a space standard, and housing is legally considered overcrowded if either of these is breached.

The room standard is breached if the accommodation available and the number of people living together means it is necessary for two people of the opposite sex, who are not living together as a couple, to sleep in the same room. Children under the age of ten are not taken into account. A room is defined as any that is normally used as a bedroom or living room. The definition of overcrowding is also affected by health and safety regulations, which state, for example, that a room with a gas fire is unsuitable to be counted as a bedroom.[63]

The space standard is breached where the number of people living together is more than a set limit according to the available number of rooms or floor space (whichever is the lower of the two). Children under one are disregarded and children under ten are counted as half a person. Rooms with floor areas of less than 4.6 m^2 are not counted. The space standard according to number of rooms available is as follows:

Total number of bedrooms or living rooms	Total number of people
1	2
2	3
3	5
4	7 ½
5 or more	2 for each room

The space standard based on floor area is:

Floor area of room	Number of people
4.6 – 6.5 m^2	½
6.5 – 8.4 m^2	1
8.4 – 10.2 m^2	1 ½
10.2 m^2 or more	2

Bedroom standard[64]

In the bedroom standard, a separate bedroom is required by each:

- Married or cohabiting couple
- Adult aged 21 or older
- Pair of adolescents aged 10-20 of the same sex
- Pair of children aged under 10 regardless of sex

Any unpaired person aged 10-20 is paired, if possible, with a child aged under ten of the same sex or, if that is not possible, given a separate bedroom. The same applies to any unpaired child aged under ten. A household is deemed to be overcrowded if they lack one or more bedrooms.

Occupancy rating[65]

The occupancy rating provides a measure of under-occupancy and overcrowding used by the UK Census. It is calculated by assuming that each household requires two "common rooms" as well as a bedroom for the following:

- Each couple
- Each lone parent
- Any other person aged 16 or over
- Each pair aged 10-15 of the same sex
- Each pair formed from a remaining person aged 10-15 with a child aged under 10 of the same sex
- Each pair of children aged under ten remaining
- Each remaining person (either aged 10-15 or under ten)

The number of rooms counted does not include bathrooms, toilets, halls, landings or rooms that can only be used for storage. All other rooms, for example, kitchens, living rooms, bedrooms, utility rooms and studies are counted. Rooms shared between a number of households are not counted.

Housing Health and Safety Rating System[66]

The Housing Health and Safety Rating System (HHSRS) is a legal mechanism for addressing overcrowding and is the main statutory alternative to the bedroom standard. This tool can be used to assess potential risks to the health and safety of occupants related to lack of space within a home. There is no clear formula for establishing whether a house is overcrowded, although the guidance states that account should be taken of the ages and relationships of household members. The guidance makes a number of statements about housing space needs, such as that small children need at least as much space as an adult. Unlike most other overcrowding measures, the HHSRS takes into account a wider range of space requirements than just simply number of people per room and sleeping accommodation, such as space for living, playing and washing in privacy.

European Union measure[67]

According to the EU measure, a person is considered to be living in an overcrowded household if the home does not have a minimum number of rooms equal to the following:

- One room for the household
- One room per couple in the household
- One room for each single person aged 18 or more
- One room per pair of single people of the same gender between 12 and 17
- One room for each single person between 12 and 17 and not included in the previous category
- One room per pair of children under 12

Appendix 2: Focus groups

The following Appendix provides greater detail about the focus group approach used in this report, which is outlined in Section 3.

Twelve focus groups were held, with 90 people participating in total (44 men and 46 women) and each group comprising 6-10 participants. The groups were held across the English East Midlands between November 2011 and May 2012.

At each stage, three different types of group were held, each made up of people with specific characteristics:

- Working-age people without children
- Families with children
- People aged over 60

These groups were selected because they were similar to those used in the Joseph Rowntree Foundation Minimum Income Standard research.[68]

Beyond these broad categories, participants were recruited to include people of different ages and ethnic groups and from different housing tenures. Participants had between them experienced a variety of housing provision including family homes, shared accommodation, hostels, halls of residence, and sheltered and supported accommodation. Although the research aimed for diversity in the composition of the focus groups, they were not, and were not intended to be, statistically representative of the wider population. The groups discussed and agreed (where possible) minimum requirements for a case study household similar to their own; so people aged over 60 developed requirements for a couple aged over 60.

Participants were advised to assume the case study households had no particular health or care needs beyond those shared by all households of that type. Although the focus groups included people from diverse ethnic backgrounds, the research did not aim to consider specific cultural needs.

The focus groups were held in three stages:

- **Stage 1: initial exploratory discussions.** This stage, comprising three focus groups (one of each household type) explored people's perceptions of space in the home and how a minimum space standard might be meaningfully described. These preliminary groups highlighted key issues for discussion. A variety of different activities (e.g. card sort exercise, questionnaire and case studies) were tested out with the groups to identify which approaches were most effective.

- **Stage 2: developing minimum requirements.** Six groups (two of each household type) each focused on developing a list of space requirements for a case study household, similar to the household type of the focus group participants. Participants were asked to consider the needs of one of three case study households: a single working-age man without children, a couple with two young children, and a couple aged over 60.

- **Stage 3: final negotiation and checking.** In the final three groups (one of each household type), the lists developed at Stage 2 were presented to groups to review, add detail and consider inconsistencies. Visual aids were used to help participants be clear about what they meant (e.g. a picture of what constituted a 'single' or 'double' wardrobe, or a children's play mat). These were images of furniture and equipment selected from a high street store catalogue.

The Stage 1 and 2 discussions took place in three cities in the East Midlands: Derby, Leicester and Nottingham. The Stage 3 focus groups were held in towns and a smaller city in the region: Chesterfield, Kettering and Lincoln.

Between groups there were sometimes differences in the final conclusions reached. For example, one group agreed that one chest of drawers was the minimum needed for a couple, while another agreed that a chest of drawers each was necessary. In order to present a single list for each case study household, some decisions about what to include were adjudicated by the researcher. Where most groups came to the same conclusion, the majority view was taken. Where groups all reached a different conclusion, a reasonable compromise was made by the researcher taking into account all views expressed.

References

[1] Parliament (2011) Housing: Overcrowding, House of Commons Library Standards Note SN/SP/1013, p. 4
www.parliament.uk/briefing-papers/SN01013

[2] Malpass, P. (2005) Housing and the Welfare State, Basingstoke: Palgrave, p. 33

[3] Orwell, G. (1937) The Road to Wigan Pier, London: Penguin, p. 53

[4] Mullins, D. and Murie, A. (2006) Housing Policy in the UK, Basingstoke: Palgrave, p. 36

[5] NICE (2005) Housing and public health: a review of reviews of interventions for improving health, London: NICE

[6] Office of the Deputy Prime Minister (2004) The Impact of Overcrowding on Health and Education: A review of evidence and literature
webarchive.nationalarchives.gov.uk/20120919132719/http://www.communities.gov.uk/documents/housing/pdf/138631.pdf

[7] NICE (2005) Housing and public health: a review of reviews of interventions for improving health, London: NICE

[8] Reynolds, L. (2005) Full House? How overcrowded housing affects families
england.shelter.org.uk/__data/assets/pdf_file/0004/39532/Full_house_overcrowding_effects.pdf

[9] Goux, D. and Maurin, E. (2005) The effect of overcrowded housing on children's performance at school, Journal of Public Economics, Volume 89, Issues 5–6, Pages 797–819

[10] Braconi, F. (2001) Housing and Schooling: The Urban Prospect, New York: Citizen's Housing and Planning Council.

[11] Office of the Deputy Prime Minister (2004) The Impact of Overcrowding on Health and Education: A review of evidence and literature
webarchive.nationalarchives.gov.uk/20120919132719/http://www.communities.gov.uk/documents/housing/pdf/138631.pdf

[12] Reynolds, L. (2005) Full House? How overcrowded housing affects families
england.shelter.org.uk/__data/assets/pdf_file/0004/39532/Full_house_overcrowding_effects.pdf

[13] Myers, D., Baer, W.C. and Choi, S. (1996) The Changing Problem of Overcrowded Housing, Journal of American Planning Association, 62 (1), 66-84

[14] This definition was retained in the 1985 Housing Act, which currently applies in England and Wales only. The equivalent definition in the Housing (Scotland) Act 1987 is almost identical. Parliament (2011) Housing: overcrowding, House of Commons Library Standards Note SN/SP/1013 www.parliament.uk/briefing-papers/sn01013.pdf

[15] Parliament (2011) Housing: Overcrowding, House of Commons Library Standards Note SN/SP/1013 www.parliament.uk/briefing-papers/SN01013

[16] Parliament (2011) Housing: Overcrowding, House of Commons Library Standards Note SN/SP/1013, p. 4 www.parliament.uk/briefing-papers/SN01013

[17] According to the English Housing Survey there were 20.7 million households in England in 2003.

[18] Pro-housing Alliance (2001) Recommendations for the Reform of UK Housing Policy, p. 10 www.cieh.org/WorkArea/showcontent.aspx?id=38462

[19] Lund, B. (2006) Understanding Housing Policy, p. 59 (Bristol: The Policy Press).

[20] Lund, B. (2006) Understanding Housing Policy, p. 59 (Bristol: The Policy Press).

[21] Housing Act 1996, www.legislation.gov.uk/ukpga/1996/52

[22] Department for Communities and Local Government (2012) Allocation of Accommodation: Guidance for local housing authorities in England www.communities.gov.uk/documents/housing/pdf/2171391.pdf

[23] Department for Communities and Local Government (2013) English Housing Survey Headline Report 2011-12, www.gov.uk/government/uploads/system/uploads/attachment_data/file/88370/EHS_Headline_Report_2011-2012.pdf

[24] Welsh Assembly Government (2009) Living in Wales, 2008 wales.gov.uk/docs/statistics/2009/091130livingwales2008en.pdf

[25] The Scottish Government (2008) Overcrowding using Bedroom Standard by LA www.scotland.gov.uk/Topics/Statistics/SHCS/LAbedroomstandard

[26] Department for Communities and Local Government (2013) FT1421: Trends in overcrowding by tenure (web table) www.communities.gov.uk/documents/statistics/xls/2176220.xls

[27] Office for National Statistics (2004) Census 2001 Definitions, p. 38 www.ons.gov.uk/ons/guide-method/census/census-2001/data-and-products/data-and-product-catalogue/reports/definitions-volume/index.html

[28] Office for National Statistics (2012) 2011 Census: Key Statistics for England and Wales, March 2011, www.ons.gov.uk/ons/dcp171778_290685.pdf

[29] Burnett, J. (1986) A Social History of Housing 1815 – 1985 (London: Methuen).

[30] Burnett, J. (1986) A Social History of Housing 1815 – 1985 (London: Methuen).

[31] HATC (2006) Housing Space Standards legacy.london.gov.uk/mayor/planning/docs/space-standards.pdf

[32] Burnett, J. (1986) A Social History of Housing 1815 – 1985 (London: Methuen).

[33] The Scottish Government (2011) Technical Handbooks Domestic, Sections 3.11 and 3.12 www.scotland.gov.uk/Topics/Built-Environment/Building/Building-standards/publications/pubtech

[34] Welsh Assembly Government (2005) Development Quality Requirements: Design standards and guidance, wales.gov.uk/desh/publications/housing/devquality/guide.pdf?lang=en

[35] Homes and Communities Agency (2008-2011) Housing Quality Indicators www.homesandcommunities.co.uk/hqi

[36] National Affordable Homes Agency (2008) 721 Housing Quality Indicators (HQI) Form www.homesandcommunities.co.uk/sites/default/files/our-work/721_hqi_form_4_apr_08_update_20080820153028.pdf

[37] Department for Communities and Local Government (2013) Housing Standards Review: Consultation, paragraph 98, www.gov.uk/government/uploads/system/uploads/attachment_data/file/230250/1-_Housing_Standards_Review_-_Consultation_Document.pdf

[38] Department for Communities and Local Government (2013) Housing Standards Review: Consultation, paragraph 114, www.gov.uk/government/uploads/system/uploads/attachment_data/file/230250/1-_Housing_Standards_Review_-_Consultation_Document.pdf

[39] Department for Work and Pensions (2011) Local Housing Allowance Guidance Manual www.dwp.gov.uk/docs/lha-guidance-manual.pdf

[40] Department for Work and Pensions (2011) Changes Made to the Use of the Shared Accommodation Rate, HB/CTB Circular A12/2011 (Revised) www.dwp.gov.uk/docs/a12-2011.pdf

[41] Department for Work and Pensions (2013) Removal of the Housing Benefit spare room subsidy in the social rented sector www.dwp.gov.uk/adviser/updates/size-criteria-social-rented

[42] Parliament (2013) Under-occupation of social housing: housing benefit entitlement www.parliament.uk/briefing-papers/sn06272.pdf

[43] For a range of articles see Guardian (2013) 'bedroom tax', www.guardian.co.uk/society/bedroom-tax

[44] National Housing Federation (2013) 'bedroom tax' www.housing.org.uk/policy/welfare-reform/bedroom-tax

[45] Disability Rights UK (2013) The 'bedroom tax': Disability Rights UK Factsheet F5, www.disabilityrightsuk.org/bedroom-tax

[46] Housing Futures Network (2011) The Impact of Cutting Housing Benefit on Underoccupiers in Social Housing www.affinitysutton.com/pdf/20111010%20AS%20Housing%20Futures%20report%20-%20final.pdf

[47] Brown, C. (2013) Full details of first 'bedroom tax' tribunal rulings, Inside Housing, www.insidehousing.co.uk/regulation/full-details-of-first-bedroom-tax-tribunal-rulings/6528701.article

[48] Inside Housing (2013) Defining moment, Inside Housing, www.insidehousing.co.uk//6528789.article

[49] Gray, A. (2001) Definitions of Crowding and the Effects of Crowding on Health: A literature review www.msd.govt.nz/documents/about-msd-and-our-work/publications-resources/archive/2001-definitionsofcrowding.pdf

[50] Wilcox, S. (2010) Dimensions of Inequality: Housing and neighbourhood standards, p. 6 www.york.ac.uk/media/chp/documents/2010/Evidence%20Analysis%20for%20the%20Triennial%20Review%20-%20inequality.pdf

[51] Lund, B. (2006) Understanding Housing Policy (Bristol: The Policy Press).

[52] Department for Communities and Local Government (2012) Allocation of Accommodation: Guidance for local housing authorities in England, summary of responses to consultation www.communities.gov.uk/documents/housing/pdf/2170127.pdf

[53] Bradshaw, J., Middleton, S., Davis, A., Oldfield, N., Smith, N., Cusworth, L. and Williams, J. (2008) A Minimum Income Standard for Britain: What people think www.jrf.org.uk/publications/minimum-income-standard-britain-what-people-think

[54] Bradshaw, J., Middleton, S., Davis, A., Oldfield, N., Smith, N., Cusworth, L. and Williams, J. (2008) A Minimum Income Standard for Britain: What people think www.jrf.org.uk/publications/minimum-income-standard-britain-what-people-think

[55] Bradshaw, J., Middleton, S., Davis, A., Oldfield, N., Smith, N., Cusworth, L. and Williams, J. (2008) A Minimum Income Standard for Britain: What people think www.jrf.org.uk/publications/minimum-income-standard-britain-what-people-think

[56] NHS Choices (2011) Getting your Baby to Sleep www.nhs.uk/conditions/pregnancy-and-baby/pages/getting-baby-to-sleep.aspx#close

[57] Burnett, J. (1986) A Social History of Housing 1815 – 1985 (London: Methuen).

[58] Burnett, J. (1986) A Social History of Housing 1815 – 1985 (London: Methuen).

[59] Burnett, J. (1986) A Social History of Housing 1815 – 1985 (London: Methuen).

[60] Burnett, J. (1986) A Social History of Housing 1815 – 1985 (London: Methuen).

[61] Reynolds, L., Robinson, N. and Diaz, R. (2004) Crowded House : Cramped living in England's housing england.shelter.org.uk/__data/assets/pdf_file/0003/39234/Crowded_House.pdf

[62] Housing Act 1985 www.legislation.gov.uk/ukpga/1985/68/contents

[63] MacMillan, R. (2012) Council 'Breached Law' by Cramming Family into Two-bed Home, 24dash, Wednesday 24 October, www.24dash.com/news/housing/2012-10-24-Council-breached-law-by-cramming-family-into-two-bed-home

[64] Department for Communities and Local Government (2012) English Housing Survey Headline Report 2010-11 www.communities.gov.uk/documents/statistics/pdf/2084179.pdf

[65] Office for National Statistics (2004) Census 2001 Definitions, pp. 38-40 www.ons.gov.uk/ons/guide-method/census/census-2001/data-and-products/data-and-product-catalogue/reports/definitions-volume/index.html

[66] Office of the Deputy Prime Minister (2006) Housing Health and Safety Rating System: Operating guidance www.communities.gov.uk/documents/housing/pdf/142631.pdf

[67] Eurostat (2010) Glossary: Overcrowding rate epp.eurostat.ec.europa.eu/statistics_explained/index.php/Glossary:Overcrowding_rate

[68] Bradshaw, J., Middleton, S., Davis, A., Oldfield, N., Smith, N., Cusworth, L. and Williams, J. (2008) A Minimum Income Standard for Britain: What people think www.jrf.org.uk/publications/minimum-income-standard-britain-what-people-think